The Beach

Rick Sampedro

Illustrated by Agilulfo Russo

Play Station 1

1 Listen and point.

2 Listen and write.

_ _ _   _ _ _   Anna   _ _ _

| Mum   Dad   Tom |

3 Write.

My family.

In my family there is ....

....

....

4 **Listen. Say the poem.**

Hi, hello, this is me.
My name's Anna.
I'm at the sea.

Hi, hello, the sea is blue!
What's your name?
Where are you?

  5 **Ask a friend.**

Hello!
My name's
....

Hi! I'm
....

What's your name?

Where are you?

3

Play Station 1

6 Listen and point.

7 Look at Exercise **6**. Listen and match.

- bucket
- waterwings
- spade
- beach
- sand
- boat
- sea
- beach umbrella
- sandcastle

8 **Point and ask a friend.**

What's this?

It's a boat.

9 **Look at Exercise 8 and write.**

A There is a .... C H A E B   A U B M R L E L

B There is a .... K B T E U C

C There is a .... T O A B

D There is a .... C S T A A D N E S L

E There are .... S D P E S A

F There are .... W I G A W T R S E N

5

Good morning! It's a beautiful day. A perfect day for the beach. Anna is happy. She loves the beach. And Carla is happy. She loves the beach, too.

Anna is in the car with Mum, Dad and Tom. They are all very happy. They love the beach.

Who is Tom? Tick (✔).
He is Anna's:

☐ father ☐ brother
☐ mother ☐ sister

But Mum and Dad are on the boat with her.
They are brave and strong and kind and warm.

Shhh, Nina. We're nearly there.

Look at Nina. Now look at Anna. Find 1 thing that is the same.

Anna is at the beach now.
There are lots of people at the beach, today.
And there are lots of beach umbrellas.
It's very hot!

Be careful, children!

What colour are the umbrellas?
Tick (✔).

☐ red   ☐ blue   ☐ yellow
☐ orange ☐ green   ☐ pink

Anna is in the sea.
The water is blue and cool.
She is very happy now.
It's not hot in the sea.

Splash!

Tom is in the sea, too. Look, he's got waterwings.
He can't swim.

Can you swim? Tick (✔).

☐ Yes, I can!
☐ No, I can't!

Nina can see the beach now. She's tired and hungry and thirsty. Mum and Dad are tired, too. But they can see the beach. Hooray!

Read and complete.
Nina .... tired.
Mum and Dad .... tired, too.

The boat is at the beach now.
Everyone is happy.
There are people with food and water.
Nina, Mum and Dad are safe.

Put the sentence in order.
is / Nina / now. / happy

Nina can see Anna. She's at the beach, too.

Hi! I'm Nina! And this is Sara. Can we be friends?

Play Station 2

 7

1 Listen and point.

2 Look at exercise **1**. Read, listen and match.

- They are in the car.
- They are at the beach.
- She is on the boat.
- They are on the boat.

3 **Listen and say the chant.**

I'm happy! I'm happy!
I'm at the beach!
You're happy! You're happy!
You're at the beach!
We're happy! We're happy!
We're at the beach!
The beach is fun for everyone!

4 **Look at the pictures. Point and mime. Tell a friend.**

You're thirsty.

You're hungry.

27

Play Station 2

5 Look and circle the correct word.

The doll is / isn't in the car.   The doll is / isn't in the sea.

The doll is / isn't on the boat.   The dolls are / aren't at the beach.

6 Listen and check.

7 Look, find and tick (✔).

A waterwings   B beach   C spade
D boat   E bucket   F sandcastle
G doll   H beach umbrella

8 Find and circle the words.

PDOLLAFCARHSPADELWATERWINGSPEBUCKETRO

29

Play Station 2

9 Look and match.

- ○ a yellow sandcastle
- ○ red waterwings
- ○ a black and white bucket
- ○ a brown teddy bear
- ○ an orange car
- ○ a grey spade
- ○ a blue boat
- ○ a green and pink beach umbrella

 10 Listen and tick (✔).

A

B

C

D

 11 Listen and colour.

 12 Look at Exercise **11**. Listen and circle the correct answer.

A Yes, I can. / No, I can't.
B Yes, I can. / No, I can't.
C Yes, I can. / No, I can't.
D Yes, I can / No, I can't.
E Yes, I can. / No, I can't.
F Yes, I can. / No, I can't.

31

Play Station Project

Sand Bottles

Make a sand bottle for your family.

You need:

sand
coloured chalks
a clear plastic bottle
wax/baking paper
a funnel

2 Pour the coloured sand into the bottle. (You can use a funnel.)

3 Choose another chalk and colour some more sand, then pour it into the bottle.

4 Repeat 2 and 3 until your bottle is full of different colours of sand.

5 Press the sand down and fill your bottle completely. Put the lid or cap on the bottle. Close tightly.

1 Put some sand on the wax/baking paper. Roll a piece of coloured chalk across the sand until the sand changes colour.

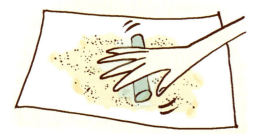

Go to www.helblingyoungreaders.com to download this page.